PENGUIN BOOKS — GREAT IDEAS

*Brief Notes on the Art and Manner
of Arranging One's Books*

Georges Perec

1936–1982

Georges Perec

Brief Notes on the Art and Manner of Arranging One's Books

Translated by John Sturrock

PENGUIN BOOKS — GREAT IDEAS

PENGUIN BOOKS

UK | USA | Canada | Ireland | Australia
India | New Zealand | South Africa

Penguin Books is part of the Penguin Random House group
of companies whose addresses can be found at
global.penguinrandomhouse.com.

Penguin
Random House
UK

Set in 11.2/13.75 pt Dante MT Std
Typeset by Jouve (UK), Milton Keynes
Printed and bound in Great Britain by Clays Ltd, Elcograf S.p.A.

A CIP catalogue record for this book
is available from the British Library

ISBN: 978–0–241–47521–8

www.greenpenguin.co.uk

Contents

Robert Antelme or the Truth of Literature*

The literature of the concentration camps does not get attacked. The moment a book speaks of the camps, or even, more generally, of Nazism, it's more or less assured of being everywhere received with a certain sympathy. Even those who don't like it won't want to say hard things about it. At worst it won't be spoken of at all. You might go so far as to say that it's indecent to link the world of the camps with what is called, if need be with a faint note of disdain, 'literature'.

Yet it seems that such an attitude is often ambiguous. The literature of the camps is most often seen merely as a useful or even necessary testimony, as a precious, indeed indispensable and upsetting document on the 'atmosphere' of the time: the war, the Liberation, the 'turning-point of our civilization'. But it's clear that a careful distinction is being drawn between books like these and 'real' literature. To the point where we no

* First published in *Partisans* in 1962. At the time when he wrote *L'Espèce humaine*, Robert Antelme was the husband of the novelist Marguerite Duras. She helped nurse him back to health but then left him for another left-wing writer, Denys Mascolo. This essay dates to a time when Perec was more political in his outlook than he subsequently became.

I

longer quite know whether underlying this attitude is the fact that we feel too great a respect (or have too bad a conscience) faced with the phenomenon of the camps, to the extent of believing that such expression as literature can give to it will only ever be inauthentic and ineffective, or whether we believe that the experience of a deportee is unable, in itself, to give rise to a work of art. We don't quite know whether it is literature that we look down on, in the name of the concentration camps, or the concentration camps, in the name of literature. However that may be, this twofold attitude accounts for more or less the totality of the actual audience and the actual impact – falsified and superficial – of camp literature.

But literature is not an activity separated from life. We live in a world of words, of language, of stories. Writing is not the privilege exclusively of the man who sets aside for his century a brief hour of conscientious immortality each evening and lovingly fashions, in the silence of his study, what others will later proclaim, solemnly, to be 'the honour and integrity of our letters'. Literature is indissolubly bound up with life, it is the necessary prolongation, the obvious culmination, the indispensable complement of experience. All experience opens on to literature and all literature on to experience and the path that leads from one to the other, whether it be literary creation or reading, establishes this relationship between the fragmentary and the whole, this passage from the anecdotal to the historical, this interplay between the general and the particular, between what is felt and what is understood, which form the very tissue of our consciousness.

For the returning deportee, to speak, to write, is a need as strong and immediate as is his need for calcium, for sugar, sunlight, meat, sleep and silence. It's not the case that he can remain silent and forget. He has first of all to remember. He has to explain, to tell, to dominate that world whose victim he was.

'In the first days following our return,' writes Robert Antelme, 'we were all of us, I think, prey to a veritable delirium. We wanted to speak, to be heard finally. We were told that our physical appearance was sufficiently eloquent in itself. But we had just come back, we had brought our memory back with us, our living experience, and we felt a frantic desire to tell it just as it was.'

This is when the problems arise. The need is to testify as to what the world of the camps was like. But what is a testimony? At the time when Robert Antelme was sitting down to write, the contents page of just about every review contained an episode, or a document, or a testimony concerning the camps. They were being recounted and made manifest in dozens of books.

But it happens that testimony can be mistaken, or can fail. In the end, people display the same attitudes towards books about the camps as they do towards the camps themselves: they clench their fists, grow indignant, are moved. But they attempt neither to understand, nor to think more deeply about them. The Americans who liberated Robert Antelme in Dachau said 'Frightful', and left it at that. And Micheline Maurel, in *Un camp très ordinaire*, tells us that the question most frequently put to her when she came back was 'Were you raped?' That was the one question that truly interested people, the only one that fitted in with their notion of terror. Beyond that there was nothing, they didn't understand, couldn't imagine. They stopped short at a facile compassion. In every case, whether it was monotonous or spectacular, the horror numbed them. The testimonies were ineffective; stupefaction, stunned amazement or anger became the normal modes of reading. But those who wrote sought to go further than that. They didn't want to evoke pity, tenderness or revolt. It was a matter of making people understand what they couldn't understand, of expressing what was inexpressible.

'Right from the start,' writes Robert Antelme,

> it seemed to us impossible to overcome the distance we discovered between the language available to us and this experience which, for the most part, we were still continuing in our bodies. How could we resign ourselves to not trying to explain how we had reached this state? We were still in it. Yet it was impossible. The moment we began to recount we felt suffocated. Even to ourselves what we had to tell then began to appear *unimaginable*. And the passage of time only confirmed this disproportion between the experience we had lived through and the account it was possible to give of it. We had to deal indeed with one of those realities which make

people say that they exceed the imagination. It was clear from then on that it was only through choice, through the imagination that is, that we could try and say something about it.

We think we know the camps because we have seen, or think we have seen, the watchtowers, the barbed wire, the gas chambers. Because we think we know the number of dead. But statistics never speak. We make no difference between a thousand dead and a hundred thousand. Photographs, souvenirs, gravestones, tell us nothing. In Munich, tourist signs invite you to visit Dachau. Huts are empty and clean, the grass is growing.

We think we know what the terrible is: a 'terrible' event, a 'terrible' story. It has a beginning, a culminating moment, an end. But we understand nothing. We don't understand the unendingness of hunger. Emptiness. Absence. The body eating itself away. The word 'nothing'. We don't know the camps.

Facts don't speak for themselves, it's an error to think that they do. Or, if they speak, we have to persuade ourselves that we can't hear them, or, more seriously still, that we aren't hearing them aright. In the main the literature of the camps has made this error. It has succumbed to the temptation characteristic of the naturalistic, historico-social novel (the ambition to paint a 'fresco'), and has piled up facts, has multiplied the exhaustive descriptions of episodes it believed to be intrinsically meaningful. But they weren't so. They weren't so for us. We were not involved. We remained strangers to that world, which was a fragment of history that had unfolded somewhere beyond us.

To get us to respond to the world of the camps – that is, to turn what had affected him into something that might affect us, and exhaust his particular experience by making it ours – Robert Antelme elaborates and transforms the facts, themes and circumstances of his deportation by integrating them into a specific literary framework, whereas the other accounts of the camps had used an elementary framework hardly differing from that of the novel. In the first place, he chose to reject any appeal to spectacle or to the immediately emotive, over which it would be too easy for the reader to pause.

He is aided in this, admittedly, by the circumstances of his particular experience, his detention having been spent for the most part in quite a minor Kommando. But his rejection of anything outsized or apocalyptic is in fact part of a determination that governs the organization of his story right down to its smallest details, and which gives it its specific colouring: a desire for simplicity, for a previously unknown everydayness, which goes so far as to *betray* the 'reality' in order to express it more effectively and prevent us from finding it 'unbearable'. Thus it is that we shall learn almost nothing, and then only very late on in the book, of what it meant for Antelme, himself still unharmed, to discover the walking skeletons that were the deportees of slightly longer standing. In every other work about the camps, this is a privileged episode, but such a sudden, limitless discovery of suffering and terror doesn't reveal the camp as it purports to do, and as it in effect *did* for the new arrivals. In the reader it can only evoke a falsified compassion that barely disguises a refusal, pure and simple.

This refusal of compassion goes further still. The world of the camp is held at a distance. Robert Antelme refuses to treat of his experience as a whole, as given once and for all, as a matter of course, eloquent in itself. He breaks it up. He questions it. It might be enough for him to *evoke*, just as it might be enough to display his sores without commenting on them. But between his experience and ourselves, he interposes the whole grid of a discovery, of a memory, of a consciousness that goes to the limit.

Implicit in the other accounts is the *evidence* of the camp, the horror, the evidence of a whole world, shut in on itself, which is restored en bloc. But in *L'Espèce humaine* ['Humankind'], the camp is never a given. It imposes itself, it emerges gradually. It is the mud, then hunger, then cold, then the beatings, hunger again, fleas. Then all of them at once. The waiting and the solitude. The dereliction. The destitution of the body, the insults. The barbed wire and the brutality. The exhaustion. The faces of the SS, of the Kapo, of the Meister. The whole of Germany, the whole horizon: the universe, eternity.

There are no hangings or crematoria. There are no ready-made images, reassuring in their very violence.

There isn't in *L'Espèce humaine* a single 'horror image'. Instead there is time dragging itself out, a chronology that hesitates, a present moment that persists, hours that never end, moments of vacancy and unconsciousness, days without a date, brief instants of an 'individual destiny', hours of abandonment: 'It seemed that midday would never come, that the war would never end . . .'

There are no *explanations*. But nor is there one fact which is not transcended, not transformed, not integrated into a much vaster perspective. Whatever the event, it is always accompanied by a becoming aware, as the world of the camp is broadened and unveiled. There is no fact that does not become exemplary. The account is forever breaking off and awareness infiltrates the anecdote, giving it density: the particular moment in the camp becomes dreadfully heavy, takes on meaning, exhausts the camp for a moment then opens out into another memory.

This continual interplay between memory and awareness, between the experimental and the exemplary, between the anecdotal tissue of an event and its global interpretation, between the description of a phenomenon and the analysis of a mechanism, this constant setting of the memory into perspective, this projection of the particular into the general and the general into the particular, these are methods specific to literary creation inasmuch as they organize the raw material, invent a style, and reveal a certain kind of relationship between the elements of the story: a hierarchization, an integration, a progression. They serve to shatter the immediate, ineffective picture we make for ourselves of the reality of the camps. Here, they appear for the very first time detached from their most conventional meanings, challenged, put to the question, scattered, revealed bit by bit through a series of mediations that go to the very heart of our response, without our being able to escape them.

The essential principle of the concentration camp system was everywhere the same: negation. This might involve instant extermination, but that in the end was the simplest case. More often, it was a slow destruction, an elimination. The deportee had to become faceless, to be nothing but skin stretched over protruding bones. He had to be attacked and worn down by cold, by fatigue, by hunger: to demean himself and to regress. He had to offer the spectacle of a degenerate humanity, searching in dustbins and eating peelings or grass. He had to have fleas, scabies, be covered in vermin. He had to be nothing but vermin himself. Then Germany would have the concrete proof of its superiority.

The SS used all known means of oppression. The commonest and most effective was to put common criminals – swindlers, murderers, sadists – in with the political deportees, so that, once mixed in with the 'bandits', the enemy, too, became 'bandits'.

The lives of a certain number of intermediaries – Lagerältester, Kapos, Vorarbeiter, etc. – were saved by the bureaucracy of the camps, where hierarchization was carried to an extreme and responsibilities were shared out in such a way as to enable a limited number of SS guards to reign over a mass of detainees. In a certain number of camps – mainly the larger ones – the political deportees were of longer standing and more self-aware and, after months or even years of struggle, they took control of the key posts. They succeeded in establishing a legal system, or form of discipline, within the system of the camp which worked against the jurisdiction of the SS because it involved a total and effective solidarity among the detainees. Directives were either not applied or diverted from their original intentions; the detainees in the greatest danger were protected; the most dangerous were eliminated.

In Buchenwald, a town of 40,000 inhabitants, the undercover international organization controlled all the activities of the camp. In Gandersheim, a Kommando of five hundred men, as in most of the small Kommandos, the common criminals carried the day.

Having common criminals in control of the camp meant that the jurisdiction of the SS was aggravated rather than frustrated. It meant, for example, that discipline was made impossible so that the Kapo could *restore* it with his truncheon, to demonstrate that he was different in essence from whoever he was beating and thereby deserved to live and even to prosper. Or, to give another example, that international solidarity was made impossible, with one nationality being set against others, French against Italians, Russians against

Poles; in the ensuing battles any sense of a common enemy was lost, so aiding the manoeuvrings of the Kapos.

'At Gandersheim there was no gas chamber or crematorium,' writes Robert Antelme. 'The horror was not on any huge scale. The horror lay in the obscurity, the complete absence of landmarks, the solitude, the ceaseless oppression, the slow annihilation.' Here we have the definition of the typical camp: this is the mechanism of the camps laid bare. The oppression recognized no limits, the deportee no refuge.

Gandersheim was the least particularized of the camps. The risks there were the most modest, the chances the least great. There were no instruments of death, no hangings, no torture. But there was nothing that might enable them to live. The political organization ensured the safety of a certain percentage of the camp's population. Rule by the criminal element meant any organization was out of the question. 'It became impossible to get a bit more food for those comrades who were sinking too fast. Impossible to hide the ones assigned to work that was too hard for them. Impossible to use the *revier* and the *schonung* as happened in other camps.'*

Solidarity is neither a metaphysical given nor a categorical imperative. It is linked to precise circumstances. It is necessary to the survival of a group because

---

* These two German terms describe the ways in which camp inmates might be spared some of its rigours on grounds of sickness, etc.

it ensures that group's cohesiveness, and it only has to be outlawed for the world of the camps to appear in all its logic. *L'Espèce humaine*, being an *everyday* description, is also the most general description of a camp. The world of the camps is defined less by an immediate, massive extermination, by 'cullings', than by days, months, years of hunger, cold and terror. The accounts given by David Rousset (*Les Jours de notre mort*) and Jean Laffitte (*Ceux qui vivent*) applied to the metropolises, to the vast sorting offices of Buchenwald, Dachau and Mauthausen, where sometimes all-powerful organizations waged an undercover campaign that was both real and effective. But there the mechanism of the camps appears in a false light. We see it through privileged eyes. We know nothing of its precise effect on an isolated individual, yet it is that effect alone that can concern us, that we can be made to respond to. Jean Laffitte's testimony in particular may remain valid at the level of a political experience – it was indispensable even, in 1947, that he should have restored it to us – but it is constantly being falsified by his populist and nationalistic glorification of the struggle, by the description he gives of the camp, by the simplistic, even mystificatory, view he takes – one chapter is entitled 'Visions of terror' and the one after that 'The good times'.

'Total oppression, total destitution,' writes Robert Antelme, 'risk casting everyone into a quasi-solitude. Class-consciousness and a spirit of solidarity are the expression still of a certain well-being surviving among

the oppressed. But although it was occasionally reawak-
ened, there was every chance of the consciousness
of the political detainees becoming a solitary one. Yet,
even though solitary, that consciousness continued to
resist. Deprived of the bodies of others, and progres-
sively of one's own body, there was life still for each of
us to will to defend.'

Survival, naturally, was a matter of luck. But luck in the
end explains nothing. In Robert Antelme's detention
there were moments he was unable to control. That he
didn't die then was attributable to good fortune, to
some purely automatic reaction, or to someone else's
unhoped-for gesture. Of other moments he remained
master and then he triumphed over death. *L'Espèce
humaine* is the story of that triumph.

'Normal' life ignores death. 'We each of us work and
eat, knowing we are mortal, but it isn't the piece of
bread in its immediacy that causes death to retreat.' It
was precisely in this, however, that the deportee was
affected. Because everything is being done to make him
die, because that is the objective chosen for him by the
SS, his life merges with the effort he makes so as not to
die. To survive and to live is all the same, in a single
willing of the body not to succumb.

Survival is in the first instance a phenomenon of
consciousness. It is an 'almost biological claim to membership of the human species', a becoming aware of
your body as an irreducible totality, a discovery of yourself as an indestructible singularity. To the omnipotent,

omnipresent necessity of death, must be opposed the necessity of life. Just as, everywhere and always, you must 'watch out for the moment of calm that comes . . . must sit down anywhere at all, settle yourself, if only for an instant,' so, everywhere and always, you must 'provoke', must 'interrogate' space, objects, other people. You must deny the jurisdiction of the SS, show it up for the joke it is, its futility, its immediate and total impossibility, its ultimate demise.

The SS guard, 'a God with the face of an old sweat', lived in a world where he was all-powerful. But that power was a delusion. The SS man couldn't do everything. The deportee soon found that he had real power only over him, the deportee; he remained without power over nature, over things. The railway trucks eluded him, and the tree-bark, and the clouds. The whistle of a locomotive was an order to which he had to submit, *just like everyone else*. He couldn't escape it, couldn't impose his jurisdiction on it.

The SS guard had no power over anything that wasn't a man. But even over men his power soon collapsed:

> The SS guard stops, he is weary. The pals are standing there. He goes up to them, stares fixedly at them. He has no desire to make them do anything else, he stares hard at them and doesn't manage to discover any other desire in himself. He has a momentary outburst and finds they are still there, out of breath but intact, in front

of him. He hasn't caused them to disappear. To stop them staring at him he would have to bring out his revolver, to kill them. He remains for a moment staring at them. No one moves. The silence has been made by him. He shakes his head. He is the stronger, but they are there, and in order for him to be the stronger they have to be there; he can't get away from that.

Everything gives the SS guard away. His powerlessness is glaring. Unable to do everything, he can no longer do anything. He is possessed. He remains powerless before language, and before memory. He has no power over Sundays, or over sleep. He can't cancel the nights altogether. He can do nothing against the west wind, against the West, against the planes flying over Germany, against the sound of the guns. He can't halt History.

The 'burning frontier' of barbed wire that divides the camp from the innocent space of the German countryside is supposed to separate two worlds. There is the normal world, normal life, the life of houses, chairs, shops, the life in which whoever says 'I'm going out' actually does so. And the other one, the forbidden world, the world of death, ruled over by the skull and crossbones of the SS badge and inhabited by abject beings, vermin, the enemies of Germany, 'bandits', shit.

But these two worlds are a lie; they won't let themselves be separated:

The obvious falsity of everything in the countryside, which we had been so aware of when
being brought from Buchenwald, now became
a provocation. That man's false respectability,
the falsehood of his unctuous face and his civil-
ian house were horrible. The revelation of the
SS guards' blind fury, displayed without com-
punction, aroused less hatred perhaps than the
falsehood of the Nazi bourgeoisie, who sus-
tained that fury, and who coddled it, nourishing
it with their blood and their 'values'.

There weren't two worlds, but only men trying des-
perately to deny other men. But it was that above all
which was impossible:

Here, animals were a luxury, trees divinities,
but we could not become either animals or trees.
We couldn't and the guards couldn't bring us
to that. And it is at the very moment when the
mask has taken on the most hideous features, the
moment it is about to become our own face, that
it falls . . . The worst victim can but acknow-
ledge that, even when exercised at its worst, the
power of the executioner can be no more than
one of the powers of man in general: the power
to murder. He may kill a man but he can't turn
him into something else.

It is this claim to membership of the species, this
awareness that our fundamental humanity cannot be

contested, which gives meaning and direction to the effort to survive, which guides it. It calls for a new sense of solidarity, no longer active, the role of the Kapos being to forbid that, but an implicit solidarity, born of what the deportees undergo *together*. It is the basis for a new relationship between the deportee and his own body, with his singularity, with his individual history (his past and his memory, his present, and his possible future), and with others. It projects the sharp light of a more universal system on to the system of the camps, the system of the exploitation of one man by another, from which can be recovered the meaning of the struggle and of its effectiveness:

> The most despised member of the proletariat is offered a rationale. He is less alone than the man who despises him, whose space will become more and more exiguous and who will inexorably become more and more solitary, more and more powerless. Their insults can no longer take hold of us, any more than they can take hold of the nightmare that we are in their heads. We are constantly denied, but we are still there.
>
> . . . The experience of the man who eats peelings is one of the ultimate situations of resistance. It is none other than the extreme experience of the proletarian condition. It is all there: the contempt first of all on the part of those constraining him to that state, who do all they can to maintain it, in such a way that this state appears to account

for the whole person of the oppressed man and thereby justifies the oppressor. On other hand, the determination to eat in order to live is to lay claim to the highest human values . . . Many have eaten peelings. They certainly weren't aware for the most part of the greatness it is possible to discover in that act. Rather they responded to it as to a crowning degradation. But to gather up peelings was not to be degraded, any more than the member of the proletariat is degraded, the 'sordid materialist' who is determined to stake his claim and will not rest from the struggle to bring about his own liberation and the liberation of all.

It was in this unity, this awareness, that the SS guards were to become lost. This it was that they were unable to understand: in a world given over to degradation, degradation became a human value. The man who still has a face, who has muscles, who eats his fill, is and can only be a murderer. Never has the *human form* of the man who has succeeded in keeping a truthful face concealed so gigantic a lie. Never have boils, sores or grey skulls concealed so great a strength: 'We were alive, we were so much detritus, but it was now that our reason triumphed. True, it didn't show. But we have all the more reason when you have less chance of seeing any trace of it . . . Make no mistake: you have succeeded in turning reason into consciousness. You have remade the unity of man. You have manufactured an irreducible consciousness.'

★

L'Espèce humaine restores to us the trace of the road that Robert Antelme travelled, and which enabled him to survive, by questioning and contesting the world of the camps. Events occurred, facts, which were ground up by time and submerged by memory. Days and nights went by, grew blurred. These were weeks and months when they walked in their sleep.

When he came back, Robert Antelme undertook to write. For his return to have a meaning, and his survival to become a victory, a coherence needed to emerge from this confused, undifferentiated, unapproachable mass, which was by turns a vast machine and a lamentable everyday experience, a coherence that might unify and rank his memories, and endow what he had lived through with its necessity.

This turning of an experience into language, and the possible relationship between our sensibility and a world that annihilates it, appear today as the most perfect example of what literature is capable of being out of all that is currently being produced in France. Writing today seems to believe, increasingly, that its true object is to mask, not to unveil. We are invited on all sides to have a sense of mystery, of the inexplicable. The inexpressible is a value. The unsayable is a dogma. No sooner are everyday gestures described than they become lies. Words are traitors. Between the lines we are invited to read that inaccessible end towards which every genuine writer owes it to himself to tend: silence. No one seeks to disentangle reality, to advance, be it only step by step, to understand. The proliferation of the world is a trap in which we allow ourselves to be snared. Its accumulated sensations exhaust reality: neither the world nor words have any meaning. Literature has lost its authority. It searches in the world for the signs of its defeat: angst oozes out from bare walls, from moorlands, from corridors, from petrified palaces, from impossible memories, from vacant stares. The world is congealed, placed between parentheses.

But it isn't possible to avoid the world. History is not, as Joyce said, 'a nightmare I am trying to wake up from'. We have no other life to live. Even if this life was, for Robert Antelme, that of the camps. It is more immediate to see the camps as a horrible world the possibility of whose existence we can never succeed fully in understanding. But it did exist. It is more immediate and reassuring to see in the world of today something that we cannot be master of. But this world exists. And the famous so-called a 'Kafkaesque' world, in which we are overquick to see a brilliant prefiguration of our great modern 'cataclysms', takes no account of it, inferring from it instead an everlasting malediction, a metaphysical angst, a prohibition bearing down on the human 'condition'. But that's not the point.

We don't have to disengage from the world or want it to elude us simply because, in given circumstances, in a history that is ours we may happen to think we will never be able to grasp it. A relatively privileged portion of our planet knows, or thinks it knows, the angst of history, of the times that stubbornly refuse to resemble the image we persist in forming of them, the angst of a monstrous technology ('will it kill off mankind?'), of memory and of time passing. But we don't put the questions that need to be put in the right way.

We are mistaken. We can dominate the world. Robert Antelme provides us with an irrefutable example of that. This man who recounts and who questions, who fights with the means that have been left to him, who extirpates their secrets from events, and refuses their silence, who defines and opposes, who restores and rewards, has given literature back a direction it had lost. At the heart of *L'Espèce humaine*, the wish to speak and to be heard, the wish to explore and to know, opens out into that unbounded confidence in language and writing that is the basis of all literature, even if, given its intentions, and because of the fate our culture reserves for what is known as 'testimony', *L'Espèce humaine* does not wholly succeed in becoming part of 'literature'. For it is language that throws a bridge between the world and ourselves, language that transcends the world by expressing the inexpressible, and establishes that fundamental relation between the individual and History out of which comes our freedom.

At this level, language and signs become decipherable once again. The world is no longer that chaos which words void of meaning despair of describing. It is a living, difficult reality that the power of words gradually overcomes. This is how literature begins, when, in and through language, the transformation begins – which is far from self-evident and far from immediate – that enables an individual to become aware, by expressing the world and by addressing others. By its movement, its method and finally by its content, *L'Espèce humaine* defines the truth of literature and the truth of the world.

The Gnocchi of Autumn or An Answer to a Few Questions Concerning Myself[*]

Across the street, three pigeons have been sitting for a long time, motionless, on the edge of the roof. Above them, to the right, a chimney is smoking; some unadventurous sparrows are perched on the top of the pipes. There is noise down below, in the street.

Monday. Nine a.m. I've already been writing this too long overdue text for two hours.

The first question is this no doubt: why have I waited until the last moment? The second: why this title, why this opening? The third: why start by asking these questions?

Where's the great difficulty? Why begin with a play on words just sufficiently hermetic to bring a smile from only a small number of my friends? Why continue with

* This short piece was first published under the title 'Auto-portrait' or 'Self-portrait' in the journal *Cause Commune* in 1972. The 'play on words' that Perec refers to is contained in the French title: *Les Gnocchis de l'automne* is a typical Perec-quian play on the well-known Greek saying *gnoti se auton*, or 'know thyself'.

a description of a neutrality just sufficiently false to give people to understand that if I got up early, it was because I was very behindhand, and that I'm uncomfortable about being behindhand, whereas it's obvious I'm only behindhand precisely because the actual purpose of the few pages that will follow makes me feel uncomfortable. I feel uncomfortable. Is the right question: why do I feel uncomfortable? Why do I feel uncomfortable about feeling uncomfortable? Am I going to have to justify my feeling uncomfortable? Or is it having to justify myself that makes me feel uncomfortable?

This can go on for a long time. It's the peculiarity of the literary man to hold forth about his own nature, to become mired in a mess of contradictions: clear-sighted and despairing, solitary yet at one with others, making fine phrases out of his bad conscience, etc. It's been going on for quite a few years now and has begun to be profitable. But all things considered, I've never found it very interesting. It's not up to me to examine the case against intellectuals, I'm not going to relapse into all that stuff about art for art's sake or commitment.*

My problem is rather to attain, I don't say to the truth (why should I know that any better than anyone else, and by what right therefore would I open my mouth?),

---

* i.e. *engagement*, or that moral, political and philosophical commitment which the Existentialist writers of the late 1940s and 1950s in France saw as the one authentic source of meaning in a human life.

nor do I say validity (that's a problem between words and me), but rather sincerity. This isn't a question of morality but of practice. It's not the only question I put to myself no doubt, but I fancy it's the only one that has proved more or less permanently crucial for me. But how to answer (sincerely) when it's sincerity I am calling into question? How to set about avoiding, yet again, those games with mirrors within which a 'self-portrait' will be nothing more than the umpteenth reflection of a consciousness that has been well pruned, a knowledge that has been well polished, a prose made docile by the pains I have taken? A portrait of the artist as a clever monkey; can I say 'sincerely' that I'm a clown? Can I achieve sincerity in spite of a rhetorical toolkit in which the series of question-marks that punctuate the preceding paragraphs was long ago classified as a figure (of doubt)? Can I really hope to extract myself by means of a few more or less subtly balanced sentences?

'The means form part of the truth as well as the result.' I've been dragging that sentence along behind me for ages. But it's become harder and harder for me to believe that I shall extract myself by dint of mottoes, quotations, slogans or aphorisms. I've used up a whole supply of them: *'Larvatus prodeo'*, 'I write in order to peruse myself', 'Open the door and see all the people',* etc., etc.

---

* A reference to an English game played with the hands. It starts: 'Here is the church' (hands upraised with fingers interlocked, representing the nave), continues with 'Here is the steeple' (index fingers pointing up), and ends: 'Open the door,

Some of them still manage at times to delight me, to move me, they still seem to have a lot to teach me, but you do what you like with them, you abandon them, take them up again, they have all the docility you demand from them.

This doesn't prevent . . . What is the right question, the one that will enable me truly to answer, truly to answer myself? Who am I? What am I? Where am I at?

Can I measure some of the road I have travelled? Have I achieved some of the aims I set myself, if I ever really did one day set myself aims? Can I say today that I am what I wanted to be in the old days? I don't ask myself whether the world in which I live answers to my aspirations, for as soon as I've answered no, I shan't have the impression of having progressed any further. But does the life I lead in it correspond to what I wanted, to what I expected?

To begin with, it all seems simple: I wanted to write, and I've written. By dint of writing, I've become a writer, for myself alone first of all and for a long time, and today for others. In principle, I no longer have any need to justify myself (either in my own eyes or in the eyes of others). I'm a writer, that's an acknowledged fact, a datum, self-evident, a definition. I can write or not write, I can go several weeks or several months without

---

etc.' (fingers unlocked, hands turned palms up, fingers raised and wiggling).

writing, or write 'well' or write 'badly', that alters nothing, it doesn't make my activity as a writer into a parallel
or complementary activity. I do nothing else but write
(except earn the time to write), I don't know how to do
anything else, I haven't wanted to learn anything
else . . . I write in order to live and I live in order to
write, and I've come close to imagining that writing and
living might merge completely: I would live in the com-
pany of dictionaries, deep in some provincial retreat, in
the mornings I would go for a walk in the woods, in the
afternoons I would blacken a few sheets of paper, in the
evenings I would relax perhaps by listening to a bit of
music . . .

It goes without saying that when you start having ideas
like these (even if they are only a caricature), it becomes
urgent to ask yourself some questions.

I know, roughly speaking, how I became a writer. I don't
know precisely why. In order to exist, did I really need
to line up words and sentences? In order to exist, was it
enough for me to be the author of a few books?

In order to exist, I was waiting for others to designate me,
to identify me, to recognize me. But why through writing? I long wanted to be a painter, for the same reasons I
presume, but I became a writer. Why writing precisely?

Did I then have something so very particular to *say*? But
what have I said? What is there to say? To say that one

is? To say that one writes? To say that one is a writer? A need to communicate what? A need to communicate that one has a need to communicate? That one is in the act of communicating? Writing says that it is there, and nothing more, and here we are back again in that hall of mirrors where the words refer to one another, reflect one another to infinity without ever meeting anything other than their own shadow.

I don't know what, fifteen years ago when I was beginning to write, I expected from writing. But I fancy I'm beginning to understand, at the same time, the fascination that writing exercised – and continues to exercise – over me, and the fissure which that fascination both discloses and conceals.

Writing protects me. I advance beneath the rampart of my words, my sentences, my skilfully linked paragraphs, my astutely programmed chapters. I don't lack ingenuity.

Do I still need protecting? And suppose the shield were to become an iron collar?

One day I shall certainly have to start using words to uncover what is real, to uncover my reality.

Today, no doubt, I can say that that's what my project is like. But I know it will not be fully successful until such time as the Poet has been driven from the city once and for all, such time as we can take up a pickaxe or a spade, a sledge-hammer or a trowel, without laughing, without having the feeling, yet again, that what we are doing is derisory, or a sham, or done to create a stir. It's not so much that we shall have made progress (because it's certainly no longer at that level that things will be measured), it's that our world will at last have begun to be liberated.

Approaches to What?*

What speaks to us, seemingly, is always the big event, the untoward, the extraordinary: the front-page splash, the banner headlines. Railway trains only begin to exist when they are derailed, and the more passengers that are killed, the more the trains exist. Aeroplanes achieve existence only when they are hijacked. The one and only destiny of motor-cars is to drive into plane trees. Fifty-two weekends a year, fifty-two casualty lists: so many dead and all the better for the news media if the figures keep on going up! Behind the event there has to be a scandal, a fissure, a danger, as if life reveals itself only by way of the spectacular, as if what speaks, what is significant, is always abnormal: natural cataclysms or historical upheavals, social unrest, political scandals.

In our haste to measure the historic, significant and revelatory, let's not leave aside the essential: the truly intolerable, the truly inadmissible. What is scandalous isn't the pit explosion, it's working in coalmines. 'Social problems' aren't 'a matter of concern' when there's a strike, they are intolerable twenty-four hours out of twenty-four, three hundred and sixty-five days a year.

* First published in *Cause Commune* in February 1973.

Tidal waves, volcanic eruptions, tower-blocks that collapse, forest fires, tunnels that cave in, the Drugstore des Champs-Elysées burns down. Awful! Terrible! Monstrous! Scandalous! But where's the scandal? The true scandal? Has the newspaper told us anything except: not to worry, as you can see life exists, with its ups and its downs, things happen, as you can see.

The daily papers talk of everything except the daily. The papers annoy me, they teach me nothing. What they recount doesn't concern me, doesn't ask me questions and doesn't answer the questions I ask or would like to ask.

What's really going on, what we're experiencing, the rest, all the rest, where is it? How should we take account of, describe what happens every day and recurs every day: the banal, the quotidian, the obvious, the common, the ordinary, the infraordinary, the background noise, the habitual?

To question the habitual. But that's just it, we're habituated to it. We don't question it, it doesn't question us, it doesn't seem to pose a problem, we live it without thinking, as if it carried within it neither questions nor answers, as if it weren't the bearer of any information. This is no longer even conditioning, it's anaesthesia. We sleep through our lives in a dreamless sleep. But where is our life? Where is our body? Where is our space?

How are we to speak of these 'common things', how to track them down rather, flush them out, wrest them from the dross in which they remain mired, how to give them a meaning, a tongue, to let them, finally, speak of what is, of what we are.

What's needed perhaps is finally to found our own anthropology, one that will speak about us, will look in ourselves for what for so long we've been pillaging from others. Not the exotic any more, but the endotic.

To question what seems so much a matter of course that we've forgotten its origins. To rediscover something of the astonishment that Jules Verne or his readers may have felt faced with an apparatus capable of reproducing and transporting sounds. For that astonishment existed, along with thousands of others, and it's they which have moulded us.

What we need to question is bricks, concrete, glass, our table manners, our utensils, our tools, the way we spend our time, our rhythms. To question that which seems to have ceased forever to astonish us. We live, true, we breathe, true; we walk, we open doors, we go down staircases, we sit at a table in order to eat, we lie down on a bed in order to sleep. How? Where? When? Why?

Describe your street. Describe another street. Compare.

Make an inventory of your pockets, of your bag. Ask yourself about the provenance, the use, what will become of each of the objects you take out.

Question your tea spoons.

What is there under your wallpaper?

How many movements does it take to dial a phone number? Why?

Why don't you find cigarettes in grocery stores? Why not?

It matters little to me that these questions should be fragmentary, barely indicative of a method, at most of a project. It matters a lot to me that they should seem trivial and futile: that's exactly what makes them just as essential, if not more so, as all the other questions by which we've tried in vain to lay hold on our truth.

Notes Concerning the Objects that are on my Work-table[*]

There are a lot of objects on my work-table. The oldest no doubt is my pen; the most recent is a small round ashtray that I bought last week. It's of white ceramic and the scene on it shows the war memorial in Beirut (from the 1914 war, I presume, not yet the one that's breaking out now).

I spend several hours a day sitting at my work-table. Sometimes I would like it to be as empty as possible. But most often, I prefer it to be cluttered, almost to excess. The table itself is made from a sheet of glass 1 metre 40 in length and 70 centimetres across, resting on metal trestles. Its stability is far from perfect and it's no bad thing in actual fact that it should be heavily loaded or even overloaded; the weight of the objects it supports helps to keep it steady.

I tidy my work-table quite frequently. This consists of putting all the objects somewhere else and replacing them one by one. I wipe the glass table with a duster (sometimes soaked in a special product) and do the same with each object. The problem is then to decide whether

[*] First published in *Les Nouvelles littéraires* in February 1976.

a particular object should or should not be on the table (next a place has to be found for it, but usually that isn't difficult).

This rearrangement of my territory rarely takes place at random. It most often corresponds to the beginning or end of a specific piece of work; it intervenes in the middle of those indecisive days when I don't quite know whether I'm going to get started and when I simply cling on to these activities of withdrawal: tidying, sorting, setting in order. At these moments I dream of a work surface that is virgo intacta: everything in its place, nothing superfluous, nothing sticking out, all the pencils well sharpened (but why have several pencils? I can see six merely at a glance!), all the paper in a pile or, better still, no paper at all, only an exercise book open at a blank page. (Myth of the impeccably smooth desk of the Managing Director: I have seen one that was a small steel fortress, crammed with electronic equipment, or what purported to be so, which appeared and disappeared when you pressed the controls on a superior sort of dashboard.)

Later on, once my work is advancing or else stalled, my work-table becomes cluttered with objects that have sometimes accumulated there purely by chance (secateurs, folding rule), or else by some temporary necessity (coffee cup). Some will remain for a few minutes, others for a few days, others, which seem to have got there in a somewhat contingent fashion, will take up permanent residence. We're not dealing exclusively with objects directly connected with the business of writing (paper, stationery, books); others are connected with a daily practice (smoking) or a periodical one (taking snuff, drawing, eating sweets, playing patience, solving puzzles), with some perhaps superstitious foible (setting a little push-button calendar), or linked not to any particular function but to memories perhaps, or to some tactile or visual pleasure, or simply to a liking for the knick-knack in question (boxes, stones, pebbles, bud-vase).

On the whole, I could say that the objects that are on my work-table are there because I want them to be. This isn't connected simply with their function or with my own negligence. For example, there's no tube of glue on my work-table; that's to be found in a small set of drawers at the side. I put it back there a moment ago after using it. I could have left it on my work-table, but I put it away almost automatically (I say 'almost' because, since I've been describing what there is on my work-table, I am paying closer attention to my movements). Thus, there are objects useful for my work which aren't or aren't always on my work-table (glue, scissors, sticky tape, bottles of ink, stapler), others which aren't immediately useful (sealing wax), or useful for some other purpose (nail file), or not useful at all (ammonite), but which are there all the same.

These objects have in a way been chosen, been preferred to others. It's obvious, for example, that there will always be an ashtray on my work-table (unless I give up smoking), but it won't always be the same ashtray. Generally speaking, the same ashtray stays there for quite some time; one day, in accordance with criteria that it mightn't be without interest to investigate further, I shall put it somewhere else (near the table on which I do my typing, for example, or near the plank on which my dictionaries are, or on a shelf, or in another room) and another ashtray will replace it. (An obvious invalidation of what I've just been claiming: at this precise moment, there are three ashtrays on my work-table, that is, two surplus ones which are as it happens empty; one is the war memorial, acquired very recently; the other, which shows a charming view of the roofs of the town of Ingolstadt, has just been stuck together again. The one in use has a black plastic body and a white perforated metal lid. As I look at them, and describe them, I realize in any case that they're not among my current favourites. The war memorial is definitely too small to be anything more than an ashtray for mealtimes, Ingolstadt is very fragile, and as for the black one with the lid, the cigarettes I throw away in it go on smouldering for ever.)

A desk-lamp, a cigarette box, a bud-vase, a matchbox-holder, a cardboard box containing little multi-coloured index-cards, a large carton bouilli inkwell incrusted with tortoiseshell, a glass pencil-box, several stones, three hand-turned wooden boxes, an alarm-clock, a push-button calendar, a lump of lead, a large cigar box (with no cigars in, but full of small objects), a steel spiral into which you can slide letters that are pending, a dagger handle of polished stone, account books, exercise books, loose sheets, multiple writing instruments or accessories, a big hand-blotter, several books, a glass full of pencils, a small gilded wooden box. (Nothing seems easier than to draw up a list, in actual fact it's far more complicated than it appears; you always forget something, you are tempted to write, etc., but an inventory is when you don't write, etc. With rare exceptions (Butor), contemporary writing has lost the art of enumeration: the catalogues of Rabelais, the Linnaean list of fish in *Twenty Thousand Leagues Under the Sea*, the list of the geographers who've explored Australia in *Captain Grant's Children*.)

It's several years now since I contemplated writing the history of some of the objects that are on my work-table. I wrote the beginning of it nearly three years ago; rereading it, I notice that, of the seven objects I talked about, four are still on my work-table (although I've moved house in between). Two have been changed: a hand-blotter, which I've replaced by another hand-blotter (they're very much alike, but the second one is bigger), and a battery alarm-clock (whose normal position, as I've already noted, is on my bedside table, where it is today), replaced by another, wind-up alarm-clock. The third object has disappeared from my work-table. This was a Plexiglas cube made up of eight cubes attached to each other in such a way as to enable it to take on a great many shapes. It was given to me by François le Lionnais[*] and is now in another room, on the shelf above a radiator, next to several other brainteasers

---

[*] A mathematician who was one of the founders of the OuLiPo, a group of writers and painters who used constraints such as maths problems, puzzles and wordplay in their art.

and puzzles (one of these is on my work-table: a double tangram, i.e. twice seven bits of black and white plastic that can be used to form an almost infinite number of geometrical figures).

Before, I didn't have a work-table, I mean there was no table for that express purpose. It still quite often happens today that I do my work in a café. At home, however, it's very rare for me to work (write) anywhere except at my work-table (for example, I almost never write in bed) and my work-table isn't used for anything except my work. (Once again, even as I write these words, this turns out to be not wholly accurate; two or three times a year, when I give a party, my work-table is entirely cleared and covered in paper tablecloths – like the plank on which my dictionaries are piled – and becomes a sideboard.)

Thus a certain history of my tastes (their permanence, their evolution, their phases) will come to be inscribed in this project. More precisely, it will be, once again, a way of marking out my space, a somewhat oblique approach to my daily practice, a way of talking about my work, about my history and my preoccupations, an attempt to grasp something pertaining to my experience, not at the level of its remote reflections, but at the very point where it emerges.

Reading: A Socio-physiological Outline*

The following pages can be nothing more than notes, a bringing together, more intuitive than organized, of scattered facts that allude only exceptionally to constituted bodies of knowledge. They belong rather to those ill-divided domains or fallow lands of descriptive ethnology once invoked by Marcel Mauss in an introduction to the 'techniques of the body' and that, ranged under the heading of 'miscellaneous', constitute emergency zones of which all we know is that we don't know very much, although we sense we might learn a great deal from them were we to take it into our heads to pay them some attention: banal facts, passed over in silence, no one's responsibility, a matter of course. But even if we think we can get by without having to describe them, they describe us. They relate, with far more acuity and presence than most of the institutions and ideologies off which sociologists habitually feed, to the history of our bodies, to the culture that has shaped our gestures and our bodily postures, and to the education that has fashioned our motor functions at least as much as our mental acts. Mauss makes clear that this applies to walking and dancing, to

* First published in *Esprit* in 1976.

running and jumping, to our modes of relaxation, to techniques of carrying and throwing, to our table manners and our manners in bed, to the external forms of respect, to bodily hygiene, etc. It applies also to reading.

Reading is an act and I wish to speak of this act and this act alone: of what constitutes it and what surrounds it; not of what it produces (the text, what we read), nor of what precedes it (writing and its choices, publishing and its choices, printing and its choices, distribution and its choices, etc.). In short, something like an economy of reading seen from an ergological (physiology, muscular effort) and socio-ecological perspective (its spatio-temporal setting).

For several decades now, a whole school of modern criticism has been laying stress on the *how* of writing: on the doing of it, on its poetics. Not on its sacred maieutics, on taking inspiration by the throat, but the black on white, the texture of the text, the inscription, the trace, the letter taken literally, work at the micro level, the spatial organization of writing, its raw materials (pen or brush, the typewriter), its supports (Valmont to the Présidente de Tourvel in the *Liaisons Dangereuses*: 'The very table on which I am writing to you, devoted to this use for the first time, becomes for me the sacred altar of love . . . '), its codes (punctuation, paragraphing, monologues, etc.), its surroundings (the writer writing, his places, his rhythms; those who write in cafés, those who work at night, those who work at dawn, those who work on Sundays, etc.).

An equivalent study remains to be made, it seems to me, of the efferent aspect of this production: the taking in charge of the text by the reader. What we need to look at is not the message once grasped but the actual grasping of the message at the elementary level: at what happens when we read, when the eyes settle on the lines and travel along them, and all that goes with this perusal. Which is to bring reading back to what it primarily is: a precise activity of the body, the bringing into play of certain muscles, different organizations of our posture, sequential decisions, temporal choices, a whole set of strategies inserted into the continuum of social life which mean that we don't read simply anyhow, any when and anywhere, even if we may read anything.

I. THE BODY

The eyes

We read with the eyes.* What the eyes do while we are reading is of such complexity as to exceed both my own

---

* Except for blind people, who read with the fingers. Except also for those who are being read to: in Russian novels duchesses with their ladies in waiting, or French maiden ladies of good family ruined by the Revolution; or else, in the novels of Erckmann-Chatrian, peasants who can't read, gathered of an evening (big wooden table, bowls, pitchers, cats beside the hearth, dogs by the door) around one of them who is reading a letter from a son wounded in battle, the newspaper, the Bible or an almanac; or else again the grandparents of Maurice, whom Daudet called on while a young orphan girl was spelling out the life of St Irénée: 'And im-med-iate-ly-two-li-ons-threw-them-sel-ves-on-him-and-de-vour-ed-him.'

competence and the scope of this article. From the abundant literature devoted to this question since the beginning of the century (Yarbus Stark, etc.), we can at least derive one elementary but basic certainty: the eyes do not read the letters one after the other, nor the words one after the other, nor the lines one after the other, but proceed jerkily and by becoming fixed, exploring the whole reading field instantaneously with a stubborn redundancy. This unceasing perusal is punctuated by imperceptible halts as if, in order to discover what it is seeking, the eye needed to sweep across the page in an intensely agitated manner, not regularly, like a television receiver (as the term 'sweeping' might lead one to think), but in a disorderly, repetitive and aleatory way; or, if you prefer, since we're dealing in metaphors here, like a pigeon pecking at the ground in search of breadcrumbs. This image is a little suspect obviously, yet it seems to me characteristic, and I shan't hesitate to take from it something that might serve as the point of departure for a theory of the text: to read is in the first instance to extract signifying elements from the text, to extract crumbs of meaning, something like key words, which we identify, compare and then find for a second time. It is by verifying that they are there that we know we are in the text, that we identify and authenticate it. These key words may be words (in detective novels, for example, and even more in erotic productions or what purport to be such), but they may also be sonorities (rhymes), page layouts, turns of phrase, typographical peculiarities (for example, the putting of *too many* words into italics in *too many* current works of fiction, criticism or critical fiction), or even whole narrative sequences.

We have to do here with something like what information theorists call formal recognition. The seeking out of certain pertinent characteristics enables us to pass from this linear sequence of characters, spaces and punctuation marks that the text first of all is to what will become its meaning once we have located, at the different stages of our reading, a syntactical coherence, a narrative organization and what is known as a 'style'.

Aside from a few classic and elementary, i.e. lexical, examples (to read is to know straight off that the word *see* denotes either what we do when we open our eyes or else where you would expect to find a bishop), I don't know by what protocols of experimentation it might be possible to study this work of recognition. For my own part I have only a negative confirmation of it: the intense feeling of frustration I have long been seized by when reading Russian novels (. . . Anna Mikhailovna Troubetskoy's widower, Boris Timofeitch Ismailov, asked for the hand of Katerina Lvovna Borissitch, who preferred instead Ivan Mikhailov Vassiliev) or when, at the age of fifteen, I tried to decipher the reputedly risqué passages in Diderot's *Les Bijoux indiscrets* ('Saepe turgentem spumantemque admovit ori priapum, simulque appressis ad labia labiis, fellatrice me lingua perfricuit . . . ').

A certain art of the text might be based on the interplay between the predictable and the unpredictable, between expectation and disappointment, connivance and surprise. To come across subtly trivial or frankly slang expressions casually strewn through what is otherwise elegantly expressed might provide one example, rather as Roland Barthes describes at the start of *Writing Degree Zero*: 'Hébert never began an issue of the *Père Duchêne* without putting in a few "fucks" and "buggers". These crudenesses didn't signify but they did signal.'

A certain art of reading – and not merely the reading of a text, but what is called 'reading' a picture, or a town – might consist of reading askance, of casting an oblique look at the text. (But this no longer has to do with reading at the physiological level: how could we teach our extra-ocular muscles to 'read differently'?)

The voice, the lips

It is thought crude to move the lips when reading. We were taught to read by being made to read out loud; then we had to unlearn what we were told was a bad habit, no doubt because it smacks overmuch of application and of effort. Which doesn't stop the cricoarytenoid and cricothyroid, the tensor and constrictor, muscles of the vocal cords and the glottis being activated when we read.

Reading remains inseparable from this labial mimeticism and its vocal activity – there are texts that should only be murmured or whispered, others that we ought to be able to shout or beat time to.

The hands

It's not only the blind who are handicapped for reading; there are also the one-armed, who can't turn the pages.

Turning the pages is all the hands are now used for.

That books these days have almost always been trimmed robs readers of two great pleasures. One is that of cutting the pages (here, were I Laurence Sterne, there would be interpolated an entire chapter to the glory of the paper-knife, from the cardboard paper-knives given away by bookshops every time you bought a book, to paper-knives of bamboo, polished stone or steel, by way of paper-knives shaped like a scimitar (Tunisia, Algeria, Morocco), like a matador's sword (Spain), like a samurai's sabre (Japan), and of those ghastly objects sheathed in simulated leather which, together with various other objects of the same ilk (scissors, penholders, pencil boxes, universal calendars, handrests with built-in blotter, etc.) make up what is called a 'desk set'). The other, even greater pleasure is that of starting to read a book without having cut the pages. You will recall (it's not that far in the past after all) that books were folded in such a way that the pages needing to be cut alternated thus: eight pages of which you had to cut, first, the top edge, and then, twice over, the sides. The first eight pages could be read almost in their entirety without the paper-knife; of the other eight, you could obviously read the first and last and, if you lifted them up, the fourth and fifth. But that was all. There were gaps in the text which contained surprises and aroused expectations.

Bodily posture

The posturology of reading is obviously too bound up with environmental conditions (which I shall look at in a moment) for it to be possible to envisage it as a subject in its own right. Yet it would be a fascinating topic for research, intrinsically linked to a sociology of the body that it might be thought surprising no sociologist or anthropologist has troubled to undertake (despite the project of Marcel Mauss's that I mentioned at the start of this essay). In the absence of any systematic study I can only rough out a summary enumeration:

reading standing up (this is the best way of consulting a dictionary);

reading sitting down, but there are so many ways of sitting: feet touching the ground, feet higher than the seat, the body leaning backwards (armchair, settee), elbows propped on a table, etc.;

reading lying down; lying on the back; lying on the front; lying on the side, etc.;

reading kneeling (children looking through a picture book; the Japanese?);

reading squatting (Marcel Mauss: 'The squatting position is, in my opinion, an interesting position that may be preserved in children. The greatest mistake is to deprive them of it. With the exception of our own societies, the whole of the human race has preserved it');

reading walking; one thinks especially of the priest taking the fresh air while reading his breviary. But there is also the tourist strolling in a foreign town, street map in hand, or passing the pictures in a gallery while reading the descriptions of them given in the guide book. Or else walking in the

countryside, book in hand, reading out loud.
That seems to be becoming more and more
uncommon.

2. THE SURROUNDINGS

*'I have always been the sort of person who enjoys reading.
When I have nothing else to do, I read.'*

Charlie Brown

One can, very roughly, distinguish between two categories of reading: reading accompanied by some other
occupation (active or passive), and reading accompanied
only by itself. The first kind is appropriate to a gentleman who is looking through a magazine while awaiting
his turn at the dentist's; the second kind to this same
gentleman once he has returned home, at ease with his
dentition, and is sitting at his table reading the Marquis
de Mogès's *Memoirs of an Ambassador in China*.

There may come times, then, when we read for the
sake of reading, when reading is our one activity of
the moment. An example is given by readers sitting in
the reading-room of a library; as it happens, a library is
a special place set aside for reading, one of the only
places where reading is a collective occupation. (Reading isn't necessarily a solitary activity, but it is generally
an individual activity. Two people may read together,
temple to temple, or one over the other's shoulder; or
we may reread out loud, for a few other people. But
there is something a little surprising about the idea of

several people reading the same thing at the same time: gentlemen in a club, reading *The Times*, a group of Chinese peasants studying the *Little Red Book*.)

Another example was, I thought, particularly well illustrated by a photograph that appeared a few years ago on the occasion of a general feature on publishing in France: it showed Maurice Nadeau,* deep in a comfortable armchair, surrounded by piles of books higher than himself. Or else a child reading, or struggling to read, the chapter of natural history that he fears being questioned on the next day.

It wouldn't be hard to multiply the examples. What seems to bind them together is that each time this 'reading for the sake of reading' is connected with the activity of studying, has something to do with work or a trade, with necessity anyway. We need obviously to be more precise and, in particular, to find more or less satisfactory criteria for distinguishing work from non-work. In the present state of things, it seems pertinent to point out this difference: on the one hand, a kind of reading, let's call it professional, to which it is important to devote oneself entirely, to make it the sole objective of an hour or a whole day; on the other hand, a kind of reading, let's call it recreational, which will always be accompanied by some other activity.

For the purpose that concerns me here, it is this indeed that most strikes me about the ways in which we read:

* Publisher and founding editor of a literary fortnightly, the *Quinzaine Littéraire*.

not that reading should be considered a leisure activity, but that, generally speaking, it cannot exist on its own. It has to be inserted into some other necessity. Another activity has to support it. Reading is associated with the idea of having time to fill, of a lull we must take advantage of in order to read. Perhaps this supporting activity is only the pretext for reading, but how can we tell? Is a gentleman reading on the beach on the beach in order to read, or is he reading because he is on the beach? Does the fragile destiny of Tristram Shandy really matter more to him than the sunburn he is busy getting on the backs of his legs? Would it not be right in any case to interrogate the environments in which we read? Reading isn't merely to read a text, to decipher signs, to survey lines, to explore pages, to traverse a meaning; it isn't merely the abstract communion between author and reader, the mystical marriage between the Idea and the Ear. It is, at the same time, the noise of the Métro, or the swaying of a railway compartment, or the heat of the sun on a beach and the shouts of the children playing a little way off, or the sensation of hot water in the bath, or the waiting for sleep . . .

An example will enable me to clarify the object of this interrogation – which you are quite within your rights, by the way, to find wholly otiose. A good ten years ago, I was dining with some friends in a small restaurant (hors d'oeuvres, plat du jour, cheese or dessert). At another table there was dining a philosopher who was already justly renowned. He was eating alone, while reading a cyclostyled text that was most likely a thesis. He read between courses and often even between

mouthfuls, and my companions I wondered ourselves
what the effects of this double activity might be, what
the mixture was like, what the words tasted of and what
meaning the cheese had: one mouthful, one concept,
one mouthful one concept. How do you masticate a
concept, or ingurgitate it, or digest it? And how could
you give an account of the effect of this double nourish-
ment, how describe or measure it?

The enumeration which follows is an outline typology
of the situations in which we read; it doesn't answer
merely to the pleasures of enumerating. I fancy it might
prefigure a global description of the activities that go on
in towns today. Into the intricate network of our daily
rhythms are everywhere inserted odd moments, scraps
and intervals of reading time. It is as if, the imperatives of
the timetable having expelled us from our own lives, we
were remembering the days when, as children, we spent
our Thursday afternoons sprawled on a bed in the com-
pany of the three musketeers or the children of Captain
Grant, and reading had come to slide surreptitiously into
the fissures and interstices of our adult lives.

Odd moments

Reading may be classified according to the time it takes
up. Odd moments would come first. We read while we
wait, at the barber's or at the dentist's (distractedly,
apprehensive as we are); when queueing outside the cinema, we read cinema programmes; in administrative
offices (social security, postal orders, lost property, etc.)
waiting for our number to be called out. When they

know they are going to have a long wait outside the entrance to the sports stadium or the Opera, the provident equip themselves with a folding stool and a book.

The body

Reading may be classified according to bodily functions:

Food. Reading while eating (see above). Opening the mail, unfolding the newspaper, while having breakfast.

Washing. Reading in the bath is looked on by many as a supreme pleasure. Often, however, this is more agreeable in theory than in practice. Most bath-tubs turn out to be inconvenient and, lacking special equipment – book-rest, floating cushion, towels and taps within easy reach – and particular precautions, it's no easier to read a book in the bath than it is, say, to smoke a cigarette. There is here a minor problem of everyday life that designers would do well to set themselves.

Bodily needs. Louis XIV held audiences sitting on his close-stool. At the time this was quite normal. Our own societies have become much more discreet. The bog remains, however, a privileged site for reading. Between the gut as it relieves itself and the text a profound relationship is established, something like an intense availability, a heightened receptivity, reading as happiness. No one, I fancy, has dealt better with this encounter between the viscera and the sensibilities than James Joyce:

> Asquat on the cuckstool he folded out his paper turning its pages over on his bared knees. Something new and easy. No great hurry. Keep it a bit.

Our prize titbit. *Matcham's Masterstroke.* Written
by Mr Philip Beaufoy, Playgoers' club, London.
Payment at the rate of one guinea a column has
been made to the writer. Three and a half. Three
pounds three. Three pounds thirteen and six.

Quietly he read, restraining himself, the first
column and, yielding but resisting, began the
second. Midway, his last resistance yielding, he
allowed his bowels to ease themselves quietly as
he read, reading still patiently, that slight consti-
pation of yesterday quite gone. Hope it's not too
big bring on piles again. No, just right. So. Ah!
Costive one tabloid of cascara sagrada. Life might
be so. (*Ulysses*)

Sleep. We read a lot before going to sleep, and often
in order to go to sleep, and even more when we can't get
to sleep. One great pleasure is to discover, in a house
where you have been invited to spend the weekend,
books that you haven't read but have wanted to read, or
familiar books you haven't read for a long time. You
carry a dozen of them off into your room, you read
them, you reread them, until it's almost morning.

Social space

We rarely read while working, except of course when
our work consists of reading.

Mothers read in town squares while watching their
children play. Loafers hang about round the second-
hand book dealers along the quays, or go and read the

daily papers posted up outside the editorial offices. Drinkers read their evening papers while having an apéritif on the terrace of a café.

Transport

We read a lot going to or coming back from our work. Reading may be classified according to the means of transport. Cars and coaches are no use (reading gives you a headache); buses are better suited, but have fewer readers than you might have expected, no doubt because of all there is to see in the street.

The place to read in is the Métro, almost by definition. I'm surprised that the Minister of Culture, or the Secretary of State for the universities has never yet exclaimed: 'Stop demanding money for libraries, *Messieurs*. The true library of the people is the Métro!' (Thunderous applause from the majority benches.)

From the reading point of view, the Métro offers two advantages. The first is that a journey by Métro lasts an almost perfectly determinate length of time (about one and a half minutes per station), which enables you to time your reading – two pages, five pages, a whole chapter – depending on the length of the journey. The second advantage is that your journey is repeated twice a day and five times a week, so that the book begun on Monday will be finished on Friday evening.

Travelling

We read a lot when travelling. A special form of literature – known as station bookstall literature – is even set aside for it. We read above all in railway trains. In aeroplanes, we mainly look at magazines. Ships are becoming more and more rare. From the reading point of view, in any case, a ship is nothing more than a chaise longue (see below).

Miscellaneous

Reading on holiday. Holidaymakers' reading. Reading of those taking the cure. Tourist reading. Reading when ill at home, in hospital, when convalescing. Etc.

Throughout these pages, I have not concerned myself with what was being read, whether book or newspaper or leaflet. Simply with the fact that it was being read, in different places and at different times. What becomes of the text, what does it leave behind? How do we perceive a novel that is extended between Montgallet and Jacques-Bonsergent? How is this chopping-up of the text effected, when our taking charge of it is interfered with by our own bodies, by other people, by the time, by the din of the crowd? These are questions that I ask, and I think there is some point in a writer asking them.

Notes on What I'm Looking For[*]

If I try to define what I've been looking to do since I began writing, the first thought that comes to mind is that I've never written two books the same, have never wanted to repeat in one book a formula, a system or a manner developed in an earlier book.

This systematic versatility has more than once flummoxed certain critics anxious to rediscover the writer's 'trademark' from one book to the next; and it may also have disconcerted some of my readers. It has earned me the reputation of being a sort of computer, a machine for producing texts. For my part, I would liken myself rather to a peasant cultivating several fields; in one he grows beetroot, in another lucerne, in a third maize, etc. In the same way, the books I've written are linked to four different fields, four modes of interrogation that may in the last resort pose the same question, but pose it in a particular perspective corresponding in each instance for me to a different kind of literary work.

The first of these modes might be described as 'sociological': how to look at the everyday. This lies behind

---

[*] First published in the *Figaro* in December 1978.

texts like *Things*,* 'Species of Spaces', 'An Attempt at a Description of Certain Locations in Paris', and the work I did with the *Cause Commune* team around Jean Duvignaud and Paul Virilio.† The second mode is of an autobiographical order: *W or The Memory of Childhood*, *La Boutique obscure*,‡ *Je me souviens*, 'Places Where I've Slept', etc. The third is ludic and relates to my liking for constraints, for feats of skill, for 'playing scales', for all the work the idea and means for which I got from the researches of the OuLiPo group: palindromes, lipograms, pangrams, anagrams, isograms, acrostics, crosswords, etc.§ The fourth mode, finally, involves the fictive, the liking for stories and adventures, the wish to write the sort of books that are devoured lying face down on your bed: *Life a User's Manual* is the typical example.

* i.e. *Les Choses*, a novel published in 1965 which gave Perec a certain fame by winning the Prix Renaudot for that year. It describes the life of a young French couple exclusively in external terms of the objects they own and those they would like to own.

† *Cause Commune* was a review, started in 1971–2, whose general purpose was to 'undertake an anthropology of everyday life', and to do so without subscribing to any ideology.

‡ A book in which Perec recounted more than a hundred of his dreams.

§ A lipogram is a text which a given letter (or letters) of the alphabet has been excluded; a pangram contains all the letters of the alphabet; an isogram contains lines with the same number of (the same) letters.

This division is somewhat arbitrary and could be much more nuanced. Hardly any of my books is altogether free from certain traces of the autobiographical (for example, the insertion into the chapter I'm writing of an allusion to an incident that has occurred that same day). Hardly any of them has been composed either without my having recourse to one or other OuLiPian constraint or structure, albeit only symbolically, without the said structure or constraint having constrained me in any way at all.

Aside from these four poles that define the four horizons of my work – the world around me, my own history, language and fiction – it seems to me in fact that my ambition as a writer would be to traverse the whole literature of my own time without ever having the sense that I was turning back or treading in my own footsteps, and to write all that it's possible for a man of today to write: fat books and short books, novels and poems, plays, opera libretti, detective stories, adventure novels, science-fiction novels, serials, books for children . . .

I've never felt comfortable talking about my work in abstract, theoretical terms. Even if what I produce seems to derive from a programme worked out a long time ago, from a long-standing project, I believe rather that I discover – that I prove – the direction I am moving in by moving. From the succession of my books I get the sense, sometimes reassuring, sometimes uncomfortable (because forever dependent on the unfinished, on the 'book to come' that points to the unsayable towards which the desire to write despairingly tends), that they are following a path, are marking out a space, are tracing a tentative itinerary, are describing point by point the stages of a search the 'why' of which I can't tell, only the 'how'. I have a confused sense that the books I've written are inscribed in, that they get their meaning from, a global image I have formed of literature, but it seems I shall never be able to grasp that image exactly, that for me it lies beyond writing, it's a 'why do I write' to which I can reply only by writing, by endlessly deferring that moment when I cease from writing and the image becomes visible, like a puzzle that has been inexorably completed.

Brief Notes on the Art and Manner of Arranging One's Books[*]

Every library[†] answers a twofold need, which is often also a twofold obsession: that of conserving certain objects (books) and that of organizing them in certain ways.

One of my friends had the idea one day of stopping his library at 361 books. The plan was as follows: having attained, by addition or subtraction, and starting from a given number n of books, the number $K = 361$, deemed as corresponding to a library, if not an ideal then at least a sufficient library, he would undertake to acquire on a permanent basis a new book X only after having eliminated (by giving away, throwing out, selling or any other appropriate means) an old book Z, so that the total number K of works should remain constant and equal to 361: $K + X > 361 > K - Z$.

---

[*] First published in *L'Humidité* in 1978.

[†] A library I call a sum of books constituted by a non-professional reader for his own pleasure and daily use. This excludes the collections of bibliophiles and fine bindings by the yard, but also the majority of specialized libraries (those in universities, for example) whose particular problems match those of public libraries.

As it evolved this seductive scheme came up against predictable obstacles for which the unavoidable solutions were found. First, a volume was to be seen as counting as one (1) book even if it contained three (3) novels (or collections of poems, essays, etc.); from which it was deduced that three (3) or four (4) or n (n) novels by the same author counted (implicitly) as one (1) volume by that author, as fragments not yet brought together but ineluctably bringable together in a Collected Works. Whence it was adjudged that this or that recently acquired novel by this or that English-language novelist of the second half of the nineteenth century could not logically count as a new work X but as a work Z belonging to a series under construction: the set T of all the novels written by the aforesaid novelist (and God knows there are some!). This didn't alter the original scheme in any way at all: only instead of talking about 361 books, it was decided that the sufficient library was ideally to be made up of 361 *authors*, whether they had written a slender opuscule or enough to fill a truck.

This modification proved effective over several years. But it soon became apparent that certain works – romances of chivalry, for example – had no author or else had several authors, and that certain authors – the Dadaists, for example – could not be kept separate from one another without automatically losing 80 to 90 per cent of what made them interesting. The idea was thus reached of a library restricted to 361 *subjects* – the term is vague but the groups it covers are vague also at times – and up until now that limitation has been strictly observed.

So then, one of the chief problems encountered by the man who keeps the books he has read or promises himself that he will one day read is that of the increase in his library. Not everyone has the good fortune to be Captain Nemo: '. . . the world ended for me the day my *Nautilus* dived for the first time beneath the waves. On that day I bought my last volumes, my last pamphlets, my last newspapers, and since that time I would like to believe that mankind has neither thought nor written.'

Captain Nemo's 12,000 volumes, uniformly bound, were thus classified once and for all, and all the more simply because the classification, as is made clear to us, was uncertain, at least from the language point of view (a detail which does not at all concern the art of arranging a library but is meant simply to remind us that Captain Nemo speaks all languages indiscriminately). But for us, who continue to have to do with a human race that insists on thinking, writing and above all publishing, the increasing size of our libraries tends to become the one real problem. For it's not too difficult, very obviously, to keep ten or twenty or let's say even a hundred books; but once you start to have 361, or a thousand, or three thousand, and especially when the total starts to increase every day or thereabouts, the problem arises, first of all of arranging all these books somewhere and then of being able to lay your hand on them one day when, for whatever reason, you either want or need to read them at last or even to reread them.

Thus the problem of a library is shown to be twofold: a problem of space first of all, then a problem of order.

I. OF SPACE

1.1. Generalities

Books are not dispersed but assembled. Just as we put all the pots of jam into a jam cupboard, so we put all our books into the same place, or into several same places. Even though we want to keep them, we might pile our books away into trunks, put them in the cellar or the attic, or in the bottoms of wardrobes, but we generally prefer them to be visible.

In practice, books are most often arranged one beside the other, along a wall or division, on rectilinear supports, parallel with one another, neither too deep nor too far apart. Books are arranged – usually – standing on end and in such a way that the title printed on the spine of the work can be seen (sometimes, as in bookshop windows, the cover of the book is displayed, but it is unusual, proscribed and nearly always considered shocking to have only the edge of the book on show).

In current room layouts, the library is known as a 'corner' for books. This, most often, is a module belonging as a whole to the 'living-room', which likewise contains a

    drop-leaf drinks cabinet
    drop-leaf writing desk
    two-door dresser

hi-fi unit
television console
slide projector
display cabinet
etc.

and is offered in catalogues adorned with a few false bindings.

In practice books can be assembled just about anywhere.

1.2. Rooms where books may be put

in the entrance hall
in the sitting room
in the bedroom(s)
in the bog

Generally speaking, only one kind of book is put in the room you cook in, the ones known as 'cookery books'.

It is extremely rare to find books in a bathroom, even though for many people this is a favourite place to read in. The surrounding humidity is unanimously considered a prime enemy of the conservation of printed texts. At the most, you may find in a bathroom a medicine cupboard and in the medicine cupboard a small work entitled *What to do before the doctor gets there.*

1.3. Places in a room where books can be arranged

On the shelves of fireplaces or over radiators (it may be thought, even so, that heat may, in the long run, prove somewhat harmful),

between two windows,
in the embrasure of an unused door,
on the steps of a library ladder, making this unusable
(very chic), underneath a window,
on a piece of furniture set at an angle and dividing the
room into two (very chic, creates an even better effect
with a few pot-plants).

1.4. Things which aren't books but are often met with in libraries

Photographs in gilded brass frames, small engravings,
pen and ink drawings, dried flowers in stemmed glasses,
matchbox-holders containing, or not, chemical matches
(dangerous), lead soldiers, a photograph of Ernest Renan
in his study at the Collège de France,* postcards, dolls'
eyes, tins, packets of salt, pepper and mustard from
Lufthansa, letter-scales, picture hooks, marbles, pipe-
cleaners, scale models of vintage cars, multicoloured
pebbles and gravel, ex-votos, springs.

2. Of Order

A library that is not arranged becomes disarranged: this
is the example I was given to try to get me to understand
what entropy was and which I have several times veri-
fied experimentally.

Disorder in a library is not serious in itself; it ranks
with 'Which drawer did I put my socks in?'. We always

---

* A famously pompous, high-minded nineteenth-century
scholar and writer, unlikely to have appealed to GP.

think we shall know instinctively where we have put such and such a book. And even if we don't know, it will never be difficult to go rapidly along all the shelves.

Opposed to this apologia for a sympathetic disorder is the small-minded temptation towards an individual bureaucracy: one thing for each place and each place for its one thing, and vice versa. Between these two tensions, one which sets a premium on letting things be, on a good-natured anarchy, the other that exalts the virtues of the *tabula rasa*, the cold efficiency of the great arranging, one always ends by trying to set one's books in order. This is a trying, depressing operation, but one liable to produce pleasant surprises, such as coming upon a book you had forgotten because you could no longer see it and which, putting off until tomorrow what you won't do today, you finally re-devour lying face down on your bed.

2.1. *Ways of arranging books*

ordered alphabetically
ordered by continent or country
ordered by colour
ordered by date of acquisition
ordered by date of publication
ordered by format
ordered by genre
ordered by major periods of literary history
ordered by language
ordered by priority for future reading
ordered by binding
ordered by series

None of these classifications is satisfactory by itself. In practice, every library is ordered starting from a combination of these modes of classification, whose relative weighting, resistance to change, obsolescence and persistence give every library a unique personality.

We should first of all distinguish stable classifications from provisional ones. Stable classifications are those which, in principle, you continue to respect; provisional classifications are those supposed to last only a few days, the time it takes for a book to discover, or rediscover, its definitive place. This may be a book recently acquired and not yet read, or else a book recently read that you don't quite know where to place and which you have promised yourself you will put away on the occasion of a forthcoming 'great arranging', or else a book whose reading has been interrupted and that you don't want to classify before taking it up again and finishing it, or else a book you have used constantly over a given period, or else a book you have taken down to look up a piece of information or a reference and which you haven't yet put back in its place, or else a book that you can't put back in its rightful place because it doesn't belong to you and you've several times promised to give it back, etc.

In my own case, nearly three-quarters of my books have never really been classified. Those that are not arranged in a definitively provisional way are arranged in a provisionally definitive way, as at the OuLiPo. Meanwhile, I move them from one room to another, one shelf to another, one pile to another, and may spend three hours looking for a book without finding it but sometimes having the satisfaction of coming upon six or seven others which suit my purpose just as well.

2.2. Books very easy to arrange

The big Jules Vernes in the red binding, very large books, very small ones, Baedekers, rare books or ones presumed to be hardbacks, volumes in the Pléiade collection, the Présence du Futur series, novels published by the Editions de Minuit, collections, journals of which you possess at least three issues, etc.

2.3. Books not too difficult to arrange

Books on the cinema, whether essays on directors, albums of movie stars or shooting scripts, South American novels, ethnology, psychoanalysis, cookery books (see above), directories (next to the phone), German Romantics, books in the Que Sais-je? series (the problem being whether to arrange them all together or with the discipline they deal with), etc.

2.4. Books just about impossible to arrange

The rest: for example, journals of which you possess only a single issue, or else *La Campagne de 1812 en Russie* by Clausewitz, translated from the German by M. Bégouën, Captain-Commandant in the 31st Dragoons, Passed Staff College, with one map, Paris, Librairie Militaire R. Chapelot et Cie, 1900; or else fascicule 6 of Volume 91 (November 1976) of the *Proceedings of the Modern Language Association of America (PMLA)* giving the programme for the 666 working sessions of the annual congress of the said Association.

2.5.

Like the librarians of Babel in Borges's story, who are looking for the book that will provide them with the key to all the others, we oscillate between the illusion of perfection and the vertigo of the unattainable. In the name of completeness, we would like to believe that a unique order exists that would enable us to accede to knowledge all in one go; in the name of the unattainable, we would like to think that order and disorder are in fact the same word, denoting pure chance.

It's possible also that both are decoys, a *trompe l'oeil* intended to disguise the erosion of both books and systems. It is no bad thing in any case that between the two our bookshelves should serve from time to time as joggers of the memory, as cat-rests and as lumber-rooms.

Some of the Things I Really Must Do Before I Die[*]

First of all there are things very easily done, things I could do as from today, for example

    1 Take a trip on a bateau-mouche

Then things a tiny bit more significant, things that involve decisions, things which I tell myself that, were I to do them, would perhaps make my life easier, for example

    2 Make up my mind to throw out a certain number of things that I keep without knowing why I keep them

or else

    3 Arrange my bookshelves once and for all
    4 Acquire various household appliances

or again

    5 Stop myself smoking (before being forced to)

[*] The written version of a radio broadcast made by Perec on France-Culture in 1981.

Then things linked to a more profound desire for change, for example

    6 Dress in a completely different way
    7 Live in a hotel (in Paris)
    8 Live in the country
    9 Go and live for quite a long time in a foreign city (London)

Then things that are linked to dreams of time or space. There are quite a few

  10 Pass through where the Equator crosses the International Date-Line
  11 Go beyond the Arctic Circle
  12 To have an 'out-of-time' experience (like Siffre)*
  13 Take a trip in a submarine
  14 Take a long trip on a boat
  15 Make an ascent or a journey in a balloon or airship
  16 Go to the Kerguelen Islands (or to Tristan da Cunha)
  17 Ride a camel from Morocco to Timbuktu in 52 days

Then, among all the things I don't yet know, there are certain ones I'd like to have the time to discover properly

  18 I'd like to go into the Ardennes
  19 I'd like to go to Bayreuth, but also to Prague and to Vienna

---

* Jean-Loup Siffre, a well-known photographer.

20 I'd like to go the Prado

21 I'd like to drink some rum found at the bottom of the sea (like Captain Haddock in *The Treasure of Red Rackham*)

22 I'd like to have the time to read Henry James (among others)

23 I'd like to travel along canals

Next there are lots of things that I'd like to learn, but I know I won't because it would take me too long, or because I know I would succeed only very imperfectly, for example

24 Find the solution to the Rubik cube

25 Learn to play the drums

26 Learn Italian

27 Learn the trade of printer

28 Paint

Then things connected with my work as a writer. There are a lot of them. For the most part these are vague projects; some are perfectly possible and depend only on me, for example

29 Write for very young children

30 Write a science-fiction novel

others depend on things I might be asked to do

31 Write the script for an adventure film in which, for example, you would see 5,000 Kirghiz tribesmen riding across the steppes

32 Write a real serial novel

33 Work with a strip cartoonist
34 Write songs (for Anna Prucnal for example)

There's one more thing I'd like to do, but I don't know where it belongs, it's to

35 Plant a tree, and watch it get bigger

Finally, there are things it's impossible to envisage from now on but which would have been possible not so long ago, for example

36 Get drunk with Malcolm Lowry
37 Make the acquaintance of Vladimir Nabokov

etc., etc.
There are lots of others for sure.
I gladly stop at 37.

'Think/Classify'*

D. SUMMARY

Summary – Methods – Questions – Vocabulary exercises – The world as puzzle – Utopias – Twenty Thousand Leagues Under the Sea – Reason and thought – Eskimos – The Universal Exposition – The alphabet – Classifications – Hierarchies – How I classify – Borges and the Chinese – Sei Shonagon – The ineffable joys of enumeration – The Book of Records – Lowness and inferiority – The dictionary – Jean Tardieu – How I think – Some aphorisms – 'In a network of intersecting lines' – Miscellaneous—?

A. METHODS

At the different stages of preparation for this essay – notes scribbled on notebooks or loose sheets of paper, quotations copied out, 'ideas', see, cf., etc. – I naturally accumulated small piles: lower-case b, CAPITAL I, thirdly, part two. Then, when the time came to bring these elements together (and they certainly needed to be

---

* First published in *Le Genre humain* in 1982.

74

brought together if this 'article' was finally one day to cease from being a vague project regularly put off until a less fraught tomorrow), it rapidly became clear that I would never manage to organize them into a discourse.

It was rather as if the images and ideas that had come to me – however shiny and promising they may at first have seemed, one by one, or even when opposed in pairs – had distributed themselves from the outset across the imaginary space of my as yet unblackened sheets of paper like the noughts (or the crosses) that a not very skilful player of noughts and crosses spreads over his grid without ever managing to have three together in a straight line.

This discursive deficiency is not due simply to my laziness (or my feebleness at noughts and crosses); it's connected rather with the very thing I have tried to define, if not to take hold of, in the topic I have been set here. As if the interrogation set in train by this 'THINK/CLASSIFY' had called the thinkable and the classifiable into question in a fashion that my 'thinking' could only reflect once it was broken up into little pieces and dispersed, so reverting endlessly to the very fragmentation it claimed to be trying to set in order.

What came to the surface was of the nature of the fuzzy, the uncertain, the fugitive and the unfinished, and in the end I chose deliberately to preserve the hesitant and perplexed character of these shapeless scraps, and to abandon the pretence of organizing them into something that would by rights have had the appearance (and seductiveness) of an article, with a beginning, a middle and an end.

Perhaps this is to answer the question put to me, before it was put. Perhaps it is to avoid putting it so as not to have to answer it. Perhaps it is to use, and abuse, that old rhetorical figure known as the *excuse* whereby, instead of confronting the problem needing to be resolved, one is content to reply to questions by asking other questions, taking refuge each time behind a more or less feigned incompetence. Perhaps also it is to designate the question as in fact having no answer, that is, to refer thinking back to the unthought on which it rests, and the classified to the unclassifiable (the unnameable, the unsayable) which it is so eager to disguise.

N. QUESTIONS

Think/classify

What does the fraction line signify?

What am I being asked precisely? Whether I think before I classify? Whether I classify before I think? How I classify what I think? How I think when I seek to classify?

S. VOCABULARY EXERCISES

How could one classify the following verbs: arrange, catalogue, classify, cut up, divide, enumerate, gather, grade, group, list number, order, organize, sort? They are arranged here in alphabetical order.

These verbs can't all be synonymous: why would we need fourteen words to describe just one action? They are different, therefore. But how to differentiate between them all? Some stand in opposition to one another even though they refer to an identical preoccupation: *cut up*, for example, evokes the notion of a whole needing to be divided into distinct elements, while *gather* evokes the notion of distinct elements needing to be brought together into a whole.

Others suggest new verbs (for example: subdivide, distribute, discriminate, characterize, mark, define, distinguish, oppose, etc.), taking us back to that original burbling in which we can with difficulty make out what might be called the readable (what our mental activity is able to read, apprehend, understand).

U. THE WORLD AS PUZZLE

'Plants are divided into trees, flowers and vegetables.'

Stephen Leacock

So very tempting to want to distribute the entire world in terms of a single code. A universal law would then regulate phenomena as a whole: two hemispheres, five continents, masculine and feminine, animal and vegetable, singular plural, right left, four seasons, five senses, six vowels, seven days, twelve months, twenty-six letters.

Unfortunately, this doesn't work, has never even begun to work, will never work. Which won't stop us continuing for a long time to come to categorize this animal or that according to whether it has an odd number of toes or hollow horns.

R. UTOPIAS

All utopias are depressing because they leave no room for chance, for difference, for the 'miscellaneous'. Everything has been set in order and order reigns. Behind every utopia there is always some great taxonomic design: a place for each thing and each thing in its place.

E. TWENTY THOUSAND LEAGUES UNDER THE SEA

Conseil knew how to classify (*classer*) fish.
Ned Land knew how to hunt (*chasser*) fish.
Conseil draws up annotated lists of the fish that Ned Land draws up out of the sea.*

L. REASON AND THOUGHT

What in fact is the relationship between reason and thought (aside from the fact that *Raison* and *Pensée* were the titles of two philosophical journals in France)? The dictionaries aren't much help in supplying an answer. In the *Petit Robert*, for example, a thought = whatever affects the consciousness, while reason = the thinking

---

* Conseil and Ned Land are characters in Jules Verne's *Twenty Thousand Leagues Under the Sea*.

faculty. We would find a relationship or a difference between the two terms more easily, I fancy, by studying the adjectives they may be graced by: a thought can be kind, sudden, trite or delightful; reason can be pure, sufficient, good, or sovereign.

I. ESKIMOS

Eskimos, I am assured, have no *generic* name for denoting ice. They have several words (I've forgotten the exact number, but I believe it's a lot, something like a dozen) which denote specifically the various aspects that water takes between its wholly liquid state and the various manifestations of its more or less intense frozenness.

It is hard, obviously, to find an equivalent example in French. It may be that Eskimos have only one word to denote the space that separates their igloos, whereas we, in our towns, have at least seven (*rue, avenue, boulevard, place, cours, impasse, venelle*), and the English at least twenty (street, avenue, crescent, place, road, row, lane, mews, gardens, terrace, yard, square, circus, grove, court, green, houses, gate, ground, way, drive, walk); but we do all the same have a noun (*artère*, for example) that subsumes all of these. Similarly, if we talk to a pastry-cook about cooking sugar, his answer will be that he can't understand us unless we specify what degree of cooking we want (thread, ball, crack, etc.), but then for him the notion of 'cooking sugar' is already firmly established.

G. THE UNIVERSAL EXPOSITION

The objects displayed at the great Exposition of 1900 were divided into eighteen Groups and 121 Classes. 'The products must be offered to visitors in a logical sequence,' wrote M. Picard, the Chief Commissioner of the Exposition, 'and their classification must answer to a simple, clear and precise conception bearing its own philosophy and justification within it, so that the overall idea may be easily grasped.'

Read the programme drawn up by M. Picard and it appears that this overall idea was inadequate. A trite metaphor justifies the leading place given to Education and Teaching: 'It is by this that man *enters* on to life.' Works of Art come next because their 'place of honour' must be preserved. 'Reasons of this same kind' mean that the 'General Instruments and Procedures of Literature and the Fine Arts' occupy third place. In the 16th Class of which, and I wonder why, one finds Medicine and Surgery (straitjackets, Cross emergency equipment lifesaving devices for the drowning and asphyxiated, rubber devices from the firm of Bognier & Burnet, etc.).

Between the 4th and 14th Groups, the categories follow one another without revealing any obvious idea of system. One can still see fairly easily how Groups 4, 5 and 6 are arranged (Machinery; Electricity; Civil Engineering and Means of Transport), and Groups 7, 8 and 9

(Agriculture; Horticulture and Arboriculture; Forests, Hunting and Fishing), but then we really do go off in all directions: Group 10, Foodstuffs; Group 11, Mining and Metallurgy; Group 12, Furniture and Interior Design for Public Buildings and Private Dwellings; Group 13, Clothing, Spun and Woven Fabrics; Group 14, Chemical Industry.

Group 15 is rightly given over to whatever hasn't found a place among the other fourteen, i.e. to 'Miscellaneous Industries' (paper-making; cutlery; goldsmithery; gems and jewellery-making; clock-making; bronze, cast iron, ornamental ironwork, chased metals; brushes, leather-work, fancy goods and basketry; leather and guttapercha; knick-knackery).

Group 16 (Social Economy, with the addition of Hygiene and Public Assistance) is there because it (Social Economy) 'must follow on *naturally* [my italics] from the various branches of artistic, agricultural and industrial production as being at once their resultant and their philosophy.'

Group 17 is devoted to 'Colonization'. This is a new grouping (relative to the Exposition of 1889) whose 'creation has been amply justified by the need for colonial expansion felt by all civilized peoples'.

The last place, finally, is occupied quite simply by the Army and Navy.

The division of products within these Groups and their Classes contains innumerable surprises which it isn't possible to go into in detail here.

T. THE ALPHABET

I have several times asked myself what logic was applied in the distribution of the six vowels and twenty consonants of our alphabet. Why start with A, then B, then C, etc.? The fact that there is obviously no answer to this question is initially reassuring. The order of the alphabet is arbitrary, inexpressive and therefore neutral. Objectively speaking, A is no better than B, the ABC is not a sign of excellence but only of a beginning (the ABC of one's métier).

But the mere fact that there is an order no doubt means that, sooner or later and more or less, each element in the series becomes the insidious bearer of a qualitative coefficient. Thus a B-movie will be thought of as 'less good' than another film which, as it happens, no one has yet thought of calling an 'A-movie'. Just as a cigarette manufacturer who has the words 'Class A' stamped on his packets is giving us to understand that his cigarettes are superior to others.

The qualitative alphabetical code is not very well stocked. In fact, it has hardly more than three elements: A = excellent; B = less good; Z = hopeless (a Z-movie). But this doesn't stop it being a code and superimposing a whole hierarchical system on a sequence that is by definition inert.

For reasons that are somewhat different but still germane to my purpose, it may be noted that numerous companies go out of their way, in their corporate titles, to end up with acronyms of the 'AAA', 'ABC', 'AAAC', etc. kind so as to figure among the first entries in professional directories and phone books. Conversely, a schoolboy does well to have a name whose initial letter comes in the middle of the alphabet, because he will then stand a better chance of not being asked a question.

C. CLASSIFICATIONS

Taxonomy can make your head spin. It does mine whenever my eyes light on an index of the Universal Decimal Classification (UDC). By what succession of miracles has agreement been reached, practically throughout the world, that 668.184.2.099 shall denote the finishing of toilet soap, and 629.1.018–465 horns on refuse vehicles; whereas 621.3.027.23, 621.436:382, 616.24–002.5–084. 796.54, and 913.15 denote respectively: tensions not exceeding 50 volts, the export trade in Diesel motors, the prophylaxy of tuberculosis, camping, and the ancient geography of China and Japan!

O. HIERARCHIES

We have undergarments, garments and overgarments, but without thinking of them as forming a hierarchy. But if we have managers and undermanagers, underlings and subordinates, we practically never have overmanagers or supermanagers. The one example I have found is 'superintendent', which is an ancient title.

More significantly still, in the prefectorial body in France we have sub-prefects, and above the sub-prefects prefects, and above the prefects, not over-prefects or super-prefects, but IGAMEs (= Inspecteur Général de l'Administration en Mission Extraordinaire), whose barbaric acronym has apparently been chosen in order to indicate that here we are dealing with big shots.

At times the underling persists even after the ling has changed his name. In the corps of librarians, for example, there aren't exactly any librarians any more; they are called curators and are classified by classes or under headings (curators second class, first class, special curators, head curators). Conversely, on the floors below, they continue to employ under-librarians.

P. HOW I CLASSIFY

My problem with classifications is that they don't last; hardly have I finished putting things into an order before that order is obsolete. Like everyone else, I presume, I am sometimes seized by a mania for arranging things. The sheer number of the things needing to be arranged and the near-impossibility of distributing them according to any truly satisfactory criteria mean that I never finally manage it, that the arrangements I end up with are temporary and vague, and hardly any more effective than the original anarchy.

The outcome of all this leads to truly strange categories. A folder full of miscellaneous papers, for example, on which is written 'To be classified'; or a drawer labelled 'Urgent 1' with nothing in it (in the drawer 'Urgent 2' there are a few old photographs, in 'Urgent 3' some new exercise books). In short, I muddle along.

F. BORGES AND THE CHINESE

'(a) belonging to the Emperor, (b) embalmed, (c) domesticated, (d) sucking pigs, (e) sirens, (f) fabulous, (g) dogs running free, (h) included in the present classification, (i) which gesticulate like madmen, (j) innumerable, (k) drawn with a very fine camel-hair brush, (1) etcetera, (m) which have just broken the pitcher, (n) which look from a distance like flies.'

Michel Foucault has hugely popularized this 'classification' of animals which Borges in *Other Inquisitions* attributes to a certain Chinese encyclopedia that one Doctor Franz Kuhn may have held in his hands. The abundance of intermediaries and Borges's well-known love of an ambiguous erudition permit one to wonder whether this rather too perfectly astonishing miscellaneity is not first and foremost an effect of art. An almost equally mind-boggling enumeration might be extracted simply enough from government documents that could hardly be more official:

(a) animals on which bets are laid, (b) animals the hunting of which is banned between 1 April and 15 September, (c) stranded whales, (d) animals whose entry within the national frontiers is subject to quarantine, (e) animals held in joint ownership (f) stuffed animals, (g) etcetera (this etc. is not at all surprising in itself; it's only

where it comes in the list that makes it seem odd), (h)
animals liable to transmit leprosy, (i) guide-dogs for the
blind, (j) animals in receipt of significant legacies, (k)
animals able to be transported in the cabin, (l) stray
dogs without collars, (m) donkeys, (n) mares assumed
to be with foal.

H. SEI SHONAGON

Sei Shonagon does not classify; she enumerates and
then starts again. A particular topic prompts a list, of
simple statements or anecdotes. Later on, an almost
identical topic will produce another list, and so on. In
this way we end up with series that can be regrouped.
'Things' that move one, for example (things that cause
the heart to beat faster, things sometimes heard with a
greater than usual emotion, things that move one
deeply). Or else, in the series of disagreeable 'things':

> upsetting things
> hateful things
> frustrating things
> troublesome things
> painful things
> things that fill one with anxiety
> things that seem distressing
> disagreeable things
> things disagreeable to the eye

A dog that barks during the day, a delivery room in
which the baby is dead, a brazier without any fire, a

driver who hates his ox, these are some of the upsetting things. Among the hateful things are to be found: a baby that cries at the very moment when you would like to listen to something, crows that flock together and caw when their flight paths cross, and dogs that go on and on howling, in unison, on a rising note. Among the things that seem distressing: a baby's wetnurse who cries during the night. Among the things disagreeable to the eye: the carriage of a high dignitary whose interior curtains appear dirty.

V. THE INEFFABLE JOYS OF ENUMERATION

In every enumeration there are two contradictory temptations. The first is to list *everything*, the second is to forget something. The first would like to close off the question once and for all, the second to leave it open. Thus, between the exhaustive and the incomplete, enumeration seems to me to be, before all thought (and before all classification), the very proof of that need to name and to bring together without which the world ('life') would lack any points of reference for us. There are things that are different yet also have a certain similarity; they can be brought together in series within which it will be possible to distinguish them.

There is something at once uplifting and terrifying about the idea that nothing in the world is so unique that it can't be entered on a list. Everything can be listed: the editions of Tasso, the islands on the Atlantic Coast, the ingredients required to make a pear tart, the relics

of the major saints, masculine substantives with a feminine plural (*amours*, *délices*, *orgues*), Wimbledon finalists,
or alternatively, here restricted arbitrarily to ten, the
sorrows of Mr Zachary McCaltex:[*]

> Made to feel giddy by the scent of 6,000 dozen roses
> Gashes his foot on an old tin
> Half eaten by a ferocious cat
> Post-alcoholic para-amnesia
> Uncontrollable sleepiness
> All but knocked down by a lorry
> Sicks up his meal
> Five-month stye on his eye
> Insomnia
> Alopecia

M. THE BOOK OF RECORDS

The preceding list is not ordered, either alphabetically,
or chronologically, or logically. As bad luck would have
it, most lists these days are lists of winners: only those
who come first exist. For a long time now books, discs,
films and television programmes have been seen purely
in terms of their success at the box-office (or in the
charts). Not long ago, the magazine *Lire* even 'classified
thought' by holding a referendum to decide which contemporary intellectuals wielded the greatest influence.

---

* A character in *The Sinking of the Odradek Stadium*, a novel by
  Perec's American friend and collaborator, Harry Mathews,
  which Perec translated into French in 1980.

But if we are going to list records, better to go and find them in somewhat more eccentric fields (in relation to the subject that concerns us here): M. David Maund possesses 6,506 miniature bottles; M. Robert Kaufman 7,495 sorts of cigarette; M. Ronald Rose popped a champagne cork a distance of 31 metres; M. Isao Tsychiya shaved 233 people in one hour; and M. Walter Cavanagh possesses 1,003 valid credit cards.

X. LOWNESS AND INFERIORITY

By virtue of what complex have the departments of the Seine and the Charente insisted on becoming *'maritime'* so as not to be *'inférieure'* any longer? In the same way, the *'basses'* or 'low' Pyrénées have become *'atlantiques'*, the *'basses'* Alpes have become 'de Haute-Provence', and the Loire *'inférieure'* has become *'atlantique'*. Conversely, and for a reason that escapes me, the *'bas'* Rhin has still not taken offence at the proximity of the *'haut'* or 'high' Rhin.

It will be observed, similarly, that the Marne, Savoie and Vienne have never felt humiliated by the existence of the Haute-Marne, the Haute-Savoie and the Haute-Vienne, which ought to tell us something about the role of the marked and classifications and hierarchies.

Q. THE DICTIONARY

I possess one of the world's most peculiar dictionaries. It is entitled *Manuel biographique ou Dictionnaire historique abrégé des grands hommes depuis les temps les plus reculés jusqu'à nos jours* ('Biographical Handbook or Concise Historical Dictionary of Great Men from the Most Distant Times up until Our Own Day'). It dates from 1825.

The dictionary is in two parts, totalling 588 pages. The first 288 pages are devoted to the first five letters of the alphabet; the second part, of 300 pages, to the remaining 21 letters. The first five letters are each entitled on average to 58 pages, the last 21 to only 14. I am well aware that letter frequency is far from being uniform (in the *Larousse du XXe siècle*, A, B, C and D alone take up two volumes out of the six), but the distribution here is really too unbalanced. If you compare it, for example, with that in Lalanne's *Biographie Universelle* (Paris, 1844), you will find that the letter C takes up proportionately three times as much space, and A and E twice as much, whereas M, R, S, T and V are entitled to roughly two times less space.

It would be interesting to look more closely at what influence this inequity has had on the entries: have they been shortened, and if so how? Have they been suppressed, and if so which ones and why? By way of an example, Anthemius, a sixth-century architect to whom we owe (in part) Santa-Sophia in Istanbul, is entitled to an entry of 31 lines, whereas Vitruvius gets only six; Anne de Boulen or Boleyn also gets 31 lines, but Henry the Eighth a mere 19.

B. JEAN TARDIEU[*]

In the sixties they invented a device that enabled the focal length of a film camera lens to be varied continuously, so simulating (rather crudely in the event) an effect of movement without the camera actually having to be moved. The device is known as a 'zoom' lens and the corresponding verb in French is *zoomer*. Although this hasn't as yet been admitted to the dictionaries, it very soon imposed itself on the profession.

This isn't always the case. In most motor vehicles, for example, there are three pedals, each of which has its specific verb: *accélérer, débrayer, freiner* (to accelerate, to declutch, to brake). But there is no verb, to my knowledge, corresponding to the gear lever. We have to say *changer de vitesse* ('change gear'), *passer en troisième* ('get into third'), etc. Similarly, there is a verb in French for shoelaces *(lacer)* and for buttons (*boutonner*), but no verb for zip fasteners, whereas the Americans have *to zip up*.

The Americans also have a verb that means 'to live in the suburbs and work in the town': *to commute*. But they don't, any more than we do, have one which would mean: 'drink a glass of white wine with a friend from Burgundy, at the Café des Deux-Magots, around six o'clock on a rainy day, while talking about the non-meaningfulness of the world, knowing that you have

* A French poet and radio dramatist, born in 1903, whose black humour and obsession with language were much appreciated by Perec.

just met your old chemistry teacher and that next to you a young woman is saying to her neighbour: "You know, I showed her some in every colour!"'

(from Jean Tardieu: *Un Mot pour un autre*, 1951)

J. HOW I THINK

How I think when I'm thinking? How I think when I'm not thinking? At this very moment, how I think when I'm thinking about how I think when I'm thinking? The words *'penser/classer'*, for example, make me think of *'penser/clamser'*, or alternatively *'clapet sensé'*, or alternatively *'quand c'est placé'.** Is this called 'thinking'?

I rarely get thoughts about the infinitely small or about Cleopatra's nose, about the holes in gruyère or about the Nietzschean sources of Maurice Leblanc and Joe Shuster.[†] It is much more of the order of a scribbling down, of a jogging of the memory or a truism.

Yet how, all the same, when 'thinking' (reflecting on?) about this essay, did I come to 'think' about the game of noughts and crosses, Leacock, Jules Verne, Eskimos, the 1900 Exposition, the names streets have in

---

* These are phrases sounding rather like *penser/classer* in French. *Clamser* is a slang verb for 'to kick the bucket'; *clapet* is a word meaning 'a valve', used familiarly in such phrases as *'ferme ton clapet!'*, meaning 'shut your gob!'; *quand c'est placé* would simply mean 'when it's placed'.

[†] Maurice Leblanc was a writer of crime novels; Joe Shuster was one of the originators of the Superman character in the United States.

London, IGAMEs, Sei Shonagon, Anthemius and Vitruvius? The answer to these questions is sometimes
obvious and sometimes wholly obscure. I would have
to speak of feeling my way, of flair, of inklings, of
chance, of encounters that are fortuitous or prompted
or fortuitously prompted: of meandering in the midst
of words. I'm not thinking but I am searching for my
words. In the heap there must surely be one that will
come to clarify this drifting about, this hesitation, this
agitation which, later, is going to 'mean something'.

It is a matter also, and above all, of montage, of dis-
tortion, of contortion, of detours, of a mirror, indeed of
a formula, as the paragraph that follows will demonstrate.

K. SOME APHORISMS

Marcel Benabou of the OuLiPo has thought up a
machine for manufacturing aphorisms. It consists of
two parts, a grammar and a vocabulary.

The grammar lists a certain number of formulas
commonly used in a majority of aphorisms. For example:
A is the shortest route from B to C. A is the continuation
of B by other means. A little A carries us away from B,
a lot brings us closer. Little As make big Bs. A wouldn't
be A if it wasn't B. Happiness is in A not B. A is a malady
for which B is the cure. Etc.

The vocabulary lists pairs of words (or trios, or quar-
tets) which may be false synonyms (sentiment/
sensation, knowledge/science), antonyms (life/death,

form/content, remember/forget), words that are phonetically close (belief/relief, love/leave), words grouped together by usage (crime/punishment, hammer/sickle, science/life). Etc.

The injection of the vocabulary into the grammar produces *ad lib* a near-infinite number of aphorisms, each one of them bearing more meaning than the last. Whence a computer program, devised by Paul Braffort, which can turn out on demand a good dozen within a few seconds:

Remembering is a malady for which forgetting is the cure
Remembering wouldn't be remembering if it weren't
 forgetting
What comes by remembering goes by forgetting
Small forgettings make big rememberings
Remembering adds to our pains, forgetting to our
 pleasures
Remembering delivers us from forgetting, but who will
 deliver us from remembering?
Happiness is in forgetting, not in remembering
Happiness is in remembering, not in forgetting
A little forgetting carries us away from remembering, a
 lot brings us closer
Forgetting unites men, remembering divides them
Remembering deceives us more often than forgetting
Etc.

Where is the *thinking* here? In the formula? In the vocabulary? In the operation that marries them?

w. 'IN A NETWORK OF INTERSECTING LINES'

The alphabet used to 'number' the various paragraphs of this text follows the order in which the letters of the alphabet appear in the French translation of the seventh story in Italo Calvino's *If on a Winter's Night a Traveller* . . .

The title of this story, *'Dans un réseau de lignes entre-croisées'* contains this alphabet up to its thirteenth letter, O. The first line of the text enables us to go up to the eighteenth letter, M, the second gives us X, the third Q, the fourth nothing, the fifth B and J. The last four letters, K, W, Y and Z, are to be found, respectively, in lines 12, 26, 32 and 41 of the story.

From which it may easily be deduced that this story (at least in its French translation) is not lipogrammatic. It will be found similarly that three letters of the alphabet thus formed are in the same place as in the so-called normal alphabet: I, Y and Z.

Y. MISCELLANEOUS

Interjections as classified by a (very second-rate) crossword dictionary (extracts):

> Of admiration: *eh*
> Of anger: *bigre*
> Of scorn: *beuh*
> Used by a carter in order to go ahead: *hue*

Expressing the sound of a falling body: *patatras*

Expressing the sound of a blow: *bourn*

Expressing the sound of a thing: *crac, cric*

Expressing the sound of a fall: *pouf*

Expressing the cry of bacchantes: *evohé*

To urge on a pack of hounds: *taiaut*

Expressing a disappointed hope: *bernique*

Expressing an oath: *mordienne*

Expressing a Spanish oath: *caramba*

Expressing King Henri IV's favourite oath:
  ventre-saint-gris

Expressing an oath expressing approval: *parbleu*

Used for getting rid of someone: *oust, ouste*